Teaching Guide to Longfellow's The Courtship of Miles Standish

with Quizzes, Project Rubrics, and Discussion Prompts

Sarah Yasin

Copyright © 2017 Sarah Yasin

All rights reserved.

Cover Image "Priscilla Mullins" by Annie Bissett, www.anniebissett.com used with permission by the artist

Table of Contents

WHO THIS COURSE IS FOR..4
ABOUT THE GUIDE...6
MATERIALS NEEDED...7
HOW TO READ THE COURTSHIP OF MILES STANDISH.....................8
CLASS STRUCTURE...9
CLASS DISCUSSION...10
    ASSESSMENTS..11
HOW TO MAINTAIN A JOURNAL..12
REFLECTIONS...14
ENGLISH GLOSSARY...16
RANDOM JOURNAL INSPECTIONS..18
OPTIONAL CLASS TRIP..19
HOW TO PREPARE LESSONS FOR THE COURSE..............................20
HANDOUTS FOR DAY ONE..22
FINAL PROJECT HANDOUT...26
HOMEWORK..27
DISCUSSION PROMPTS...31
QUIZZES...39
FINAL EXAMINATION...49
ANSWER KEY TO QUIZZES...51
FINAL EXAM ANSWER KEY..53
PROJECTS..54
FINAL PROJECT– THE JOURNAL...65
OTHER OPTIONAL PROJECTS..66
FINAL THOUGHTS...69

WHO THIS COURSE IS FOR

Socrates taught "Know Thyself." We read literature in order to know and understand the human condition. The Courtship of Miles Standish is a work that exemplifies the struggles and triumphs stemming from our human nature.

This guidebook is intended for Catholic classrooms of all types: parochial, independent, and homeschools. The lessons are thorough and require active participation on the part of the instructor to guide students into deepening their appreciation of the poem and explore their knowledge of Christian teachings.

This course is not recommended for self-study because assessment resides in the fullness of the students' written reflections. There is an empirical difference between handing over a list of tasks for a student to accomplish independently, and checking in to review the life-lessons and questions that arise from it. The answers to all the quizzes are included, but instructors are urged to do the work along with the students in order to provide the fullest understanding of the material. This means that instructors will keep a composition-book journal and do the assignments along with the students, looking up definitions and organizing reflections in the designated sections.

Longfellow divided the text of The Courtship of Miles Standish into nine parts. These lessons are broken into palatable chunks so a class can meet twice a week, and concentrate on one part of the poem text per class. Along with an introduction, this guide offers five weeks of study. An intensive alternative is to meet daily, which can be accomplished in two weeks. Classes should be held for 90 minutes at a time.

Marcus Aurelius said to look at things for what they are in themselves. This approach is the spirit of these lesson plans. Little outside information is included on surrounding trends in historical evaluation of the poem. Rather, this is a deep seminar into the language and meaning of the poem itself.

Quizzes are meant to gauge whether students are keeping up with the readings and looking up vocabulary, and can be offered at the end of class discussions. The suggested projects are provided as supplements to enhance learning and can be assigned according to the instructor's preferences.

The style of deep reading and reflection is intended to provide two outcomes: to maximize appreciation of the poem, and to engender life-long study habits whereby writing thoughtful notes attend a serious examination of the material.

Much effort is required for this course. However, students and instructors will find the work they put into it rewarding and enjoyable.

May the Holy Spirit bless all who take this course.

ABOUT THE GUIDE

This guide follows a classical model for learning with no outside material. A study of the poem should first bring an appreciation of the poem itself. If that inspires students to explore more on their own or dedicate themselves to scholarly investigations beyond the scope of the work, that would be the mark of a successful classroom experience.

The guide includes quizzes, optional handouts, pre-reading homework assignments, sample reflection prompts for class discussion, project rubrics, and a final examination.

Students' routine of daily study, of reading assigned sections of the poem, looking up definitions, and composing reflections will take about an hour of work outside the class discussions. The class is a supplement to the work students put into reading and understanding the poem itself, and its pace is set by the instructor. Frequency of meeting is up to the teacher, but for the sake of retention it's suggested that the class convene at least twice a week to cover one section of the poem per class.

MATERIALS NEEDED

Students need only three things:
- a copy of The Courtship of Miles Standish to read from
- a blank composition book to make notes in.
- a bible

Sticky flags for tabs are recommended to keep the sections of the comp book divided. A supplemental binder is recommended to organize handouts, homework, and research. It is recommended that all students read from the same edition of the poem, ideally one with line numbers for easy location of verses. Projects require basic materials such as poster-board, markers, an atlas, scissors, glue, etc. The assigning of projects is up to the judgment of the instructor as to what will enhance learning and where it fits into the dynamic of the class as a whole.

HOW TO READ THE COURTSHIP OF MILES STANDISH

Students will be challenged to go beyond the method of reading they first learned when they were small. Instead of skipping over words they don't know, in this course students will stop and study unknown words.

READ THREE TIMES

Every reading assignment should come with a reminder to read three times:

- 1st time – skipping unknown words to get a sense of the content

- 2nd time – going back and looking up unfamiliar vocabulary and writing down definitions in the journal

- 3rd time – re-reading the passage with an eye for its deeper meaning, symbolism, and how it connects to Christian living.

Among the outcomes of this course, students will develop the habit of re-reading materials for deeper study and enrichment.

CLASS STRUCTURE

Classes can be used as a time to review the readings, proctor quizzes, and discuss reflections. Depending on their teaching style, instructors may wish to use class time to supplement the readings, take turns reading ahead aloud, or offer workshops to complete projects. This course is set up to be flexible; however, a suggested lesson plan is this:

1. Select a student to briefly summarize the text.

2. Verbally quiz students on English vocabulary using the entries the instructor has made in his own journal.

3. Review the reading. Have students recite important passages. Instructors may assign particular lines to memorize, or simply have them read aloud during class.

4. Discuss issues with and questions on the text.

5. Discuss reflections.

6. Administer quizzes, inspect journals, assign pre-reading homework.

7. Present projects.

CLASS DISCUSSION

For a seminar like this, it is recommended to be seated around a table to engage active discussion. Class participation scores should not be based on making comments and waiting for others to finish speaking until points for another comment can be added to the teacher's log; a true discussion is one where all voices are heard and reflected on. This type of class is enhanced by students working as a team rather than in a vacuum.

Discussions should begin with a basic summary of the section covered in the lesson. This is an opportunity for students to improve their class participation score, so it's recommended a different student is called on to summarize the text each time. Summaries should only take up a small fraction of class time since students are expected to complete the readings on their own before class begins.

ASSESSMENTS

1. Daily quizzes are provided to assess students' comprehension of the text as well as their diligence in defining unknown English vocabulary. Instructors need not administer them on paper, but may wish to ask the questions orally.

2. Instructors should review the quiz questions with students in class. They can be used as lesson plans (along with the Reflection Prompts) and then administered at the end of class to assess student's intellectual engagement.

3. A final examination is included in this guide, along with the final project which entails handing in the comp-book journal for inspection.

4. Along with pre-reading homework assignments, students may be graded on their participation in class discussions.

5. Projects are provided for optional use with rubrics for fair grading. A list of additional project suggestions is provided at the end of the project section of the guide.

HOW TO MAINTAIN A JOURNAL

Beginning using only the right side pages and keeping the backs blank, students (and the instructor) are expected to divide a composition book into these sections using tabs:

1. Cover page

2. Characters (allot 7 pages, skipping four lines between names to fill in definitions as the story unfolds)

3. Articles of clothing and armor (allot 7 pages)

4. Weapons for hunting and warfare (allot 7 pages)

5. Place names (countries, cities – allot 7 pages)

6. Fauna and fauna found in the poem (for an optional project – allot 7 pages)

7. Nautical terms (allot 7 pages)

8. Class notes (allot 18 pages)

9. Reflections (allot the remainder of the book for these)

10. English Vocab (beginning on the last page, label it Glossary, and fill in words neatly going from back pages toward the front, using the left side of the pages)

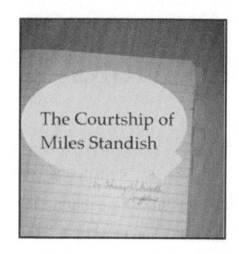
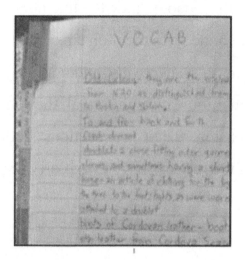
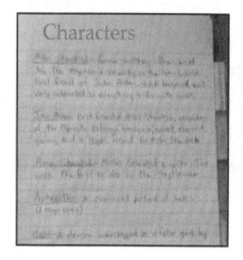

REFLECTIONS

Students may use the "collect and connect" method for writing reflections. Using the pre-printed blue line of the margin in their composition books, or drawing a line down one quarter of the length of the page to divide it, students can copy the verse they "collect" to reflect on into these segments. Be sure they also include the line number(s). On the larger side, they can write how that passage connects to them on a personal level. It's important that students reflect on the poem introspectively, and not in a general sense. Because this course is for students in middle or high school, they should already be past the point of basic reading comprehension. Their "connections" should not be mere summaries of the text. The purpose of the reflections is to explore the poem and make meaningful connections.

Personal connections can come from any of the six classical faculties of the soul:

1. Memory

2. Will (desire)

3. Perception (the senses)

4. Reason

5. Intuition

6. Imagination

One of the distinguishing features of Christianity is the call for transparency. If students open their hearts to learning from the poem, they will find treasures of God within themselves.

Students who are tempted to summarize instead of offering honest reflections do so for two reasons. The first is to avoid failure in the classroom: summaries are low-risk for students who seek approval and validation from their teachers. The second is to avoid private thought. While the privacy of students is sacrosanct, they should flex their cerebral muscles in order to show a little of themselves to others. This transparency is key for becoming a good Christian. We must always uphold the dignity of the human person and not keep the light within us a secret.

The word educate comes from the Latin *ex + ducere* (to lead out). Instructors ought to use the reflections to draw out the riches students have within themselves. Students who are reluctant to write content-rich entries should be given individualized attention. According to their own gifts, they will improve with guidance.

A final caveat: do not mistake length for content. Some students, in an attempt to please the instructor, may write long passages thinking they are being scholarly. If these passages are not personal, they are not tapping into the wellspring of their soul. Please use the list of the faculties above to aid those students who do not understand how to personalize their connection to the poem.

ENGLISH GLOSSARY

Students are required to keep a tally of words they are unfamiliar with along with words whose meanings they're iffy on. This section of the journal, located on the back page and going backward through the journal, is to be labeled GLOSSARY and the sections of the poem should be noted at the top of each batch of entries. For reference, line numbers should be noted in the margins.

Some students do not wish to expose their ignorance and prefer to pretend they know the words. Their folly will be exposed in class if they shirk their duty out of pride. The exercise of showing the limits of their vocabulary is not shameful in any way – the more words they write in the glossary section the better because it shows their openness to learning. The instructor must make it clear that no one will be docked a grade for showing they were unfamiliar with a word. By looking up every unknown word they come across, students will find how much they didn't know – and they will gain a healthy humility when approaching their studies.

Even words which seem easy to define, like "bullet," can be challenging. Some students will skip over looking up such words, but will find in class that "the thing that comes out of a gun" is less succinct than "a projectile for firing from a firearm." They will learn soon enough that words they think they know need to be given attention. Such practice will improve their rhetorical skills.

It's important the instructor keep a journal as well, writing down the definitions of words he suspects the students might not know. Use this list in every lesson to review definitions. You may wish to go around the room and quiz students orally on definitions. In the beginning of the course it's recommended not to require that students have all definitions memorized before class, but instead use this exercise to assess whether they're writing definitions down. This is part of the discipline of reading three times. Allowing students to refer to their journals during an oral quiz enforces the discipline of study this course in intended for, and builds confidence in students concerned with "getting it right."

Keep dictionaries on hand during class for questions on etymologies. It's amazing how many words we think we know when in fact we assume we know the meanings from the sounds of them and the context of the poem: stopping to look them up is an eye-opener.

RANDOM JOURNAL INSPECTIONS

Ensure students are staying on top of reflections and definitions by inspecting their journals during testing or quizzes. It's better to do this in class so they have access to the journals outside of class. One never knows when the urge to write a reflection will come.

It's recommended to devote the first class session to an introduction on scansion (see instructions for the First Day of the course) along with the housekeeping requirements for the journals. The first assignment can be as light as setting up the journal, dividing it into the proper sections, and completing the first pre-reading assignment found in the Homework section of this guide. Let the students know their first journal inspection will happen during the second class session.

It is helpful for the instructor to have already completed his journal before the course begins. The students may refer to it as a prototype to ensure they're setting theirs up correctly.

OPTIONAL CLASS TRIP

Should it be decided to include a class trip in the syllabus, please add that to Handout 1 in the grading section. Grading for a trip should be based on the preparations made, the decorum of the students on the trip, and a final thank-you note to the custodian of the location visited.

HOW TO PREPARE LESSONS FOR THE COURSE

1. Determine a calendar of due dates based on the projects listed at the end of the guide, and the availability of places to visit on field trips.

2. Read the text using a journal exactly the same way the students are expected to use it, with the same divisions and tallies of vocab and reflections

3. Incorporate the discussion prompts with your own reflections for class discussion

4. Photo-copy quizzes and use them as discussion points

5. Review the Homework and Projects section of the guide to see what should be assigned.

This is a lot of work on the part of the instructor but the rewards are abundant. Remember to ask on the final day of class for a final journal entry on the students' closing thoughts and overall opinion of the course. You will find gratitude where you least expect it in these entries. Students will tell you the English vocab they thought they knew was dwarfed by the exercises. They will write that projects brought them closer to their peers and an understanding of American cultural history. You will see them open their hearts to the light of Christ. You might find, as I have in giving this course, students declare this course to be the most enjoyable class of the year. Hard work pays off. Students will learn the more they put into their studies, the more they get out of them.

Fellowship in the Classroom

This course of study requires a deep commitment from the instructor to be closely involved with the students. One cannot simply assign tasks and expect to "follow along." Preparation and dedication are required to make this course successful and meaningful to students, and the rewards are great.

Keep in mind the beauty of the poem comes out when guided by the Holy Spirit. Every lesson is catechetical in nature, and the possibilities for edification are endless when instructors keep Christ at the center of the classroom.

Many prompts are provided with the suggested discussion/reflection questions which steer students toward Christ. These prompts may be enhanced by instructors' special gifts of teaching and the creative power of the Holy Spirit.

HANDOUTS FOR DAY ONE

The first day of class may be spent introducing the coursework. Instructors can demonstrate how journals are expected to be set up using their own journal as a model. Refer to the section in this guide on for detailed instructions.

The following handouts are for use in the classroom on the first day. Included is the rubric for the journal which students will turn in for grading at the end of the course.

Due dates for major projects can be announced on the first day. You may read the first few pages of the text together as a class, taking time to convey instructions on how to read the text three times (refer to HOW TO READ THE COURTSHIP OF MILES STANDISH in this Guide).

This is a good time to show students where to divide their composition books, and begin noting vocab, characters, and place names in the appropriate places. Advise students of the extra time they will need to spend maintaining their journals. Refer to the section in this Guide called CLASS STRUCTURE for a suggested daily lesson plan following the first day of housekeeping and scansion work.

Handout: Meter

The Courtship of Miles Standish is written in Dactylic Hexameter: six feet of dactyls. The meter can sometimes substitute spondees or trochees for dactlys, and scanning the poem requires a careful ear for the stresses.

Dactylos is Greek for "finger" – if you look at your index fingers, beginning at the palm, the joints follow a pattern: a long section followed by two small sections. This is same the pattern of a poetic dactyl: one stressed syllable followed by two unstressed syllables. Examples of dactylic words in English are: beautiful, terrible, elegant, and poetry.

- A dactyl is scanned thus:

    — ᴗ ᴗ

A **spondee** is a metric foot with two equally stressed syllables. Examples of spondaic words in English are: downtown, hubbub, and shoelace.

- A spondee is scanned thus:

    — —

A **trochee** is a stressed syllable followed by an unstressed syllable. Examples of trochaic words are: little, bumble, hobby, and leather. Most American first names are trochees (e.g. Hannah, Joey, Molly, Shawna, Hilda, Georgie, Vincent, Kathy, Sally, Timmy, etc.)

- A trochee is scanned thus:

    — ᴗ

Scansion worksheet

Try your hand at scanning for meter. Mark off the stressed and unstressed syllables with the following diacritics:

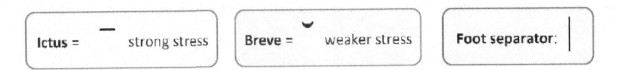

Here is a sample couplet with the scansion marked:

```
 ‾ ⌣ ⌣  ‾ ⌣ ‾   ⌣  ‾ ⌣ ‾   ⌣ ⌣  ‾ ‾
Into the open air John Alden perplexed and bewildered,
 ‾  ⌣ ⌣  ‾ ⌣  ‾  ⌣  ‾  ⌣ ⌣  ‾  ⌣ ⌣  ‾ ‾
Rushed like a man insane, and wandered alone by the sea-side
```

Scan the following couplets in pencil, beginning with the accented syllables, and finishing by marking off the feet. Be sure each line has six feet.

1. Was it for this I have followed the flying feet and the shadow

   Over the wintry sea, to the desolate shores of New England?

2. But his pride overmastered the nobler nature within him,--

   Pride, and the sense of his wrong, and the burning fire of the insult.

3. Is it a phantom of air,--a bodiless, spectral illusion?

   Is it a ghost from the grave, that has come to forbid the betrothal?

Scansion worksheet answer key

1.

— ᴗ ᴗ — ᴗ ᴗ — ᴗ ᴗ — ᴗ — ᴗ ᴗ — —
Was it for this I have followed the flying feet and the shadow

— ᴗ ᴗ — ᴗ ᴗ — ᴗ — ᴗ ᴗ — ᴗ ᴗ — —
Over the wintry sea, to the desolate shores of New England?

2.

— ᴗ — ᴗ ᴗ — ᴗ ᴗ — — — ᴗ ᴗ — —
But his pride overmastered the nobler nature within him,--

— ᴗ ᴗ — ᴗ ᴗ — ᴗ ᴗ — ᴗ — ᴗ ᴗ — —
Pride, and the sense of his wrong, and the burning fire of the insult.

3.

— ᴗ ᴗ — ᴗ ᴗ — — — ᴗ ᴗ — ᴗ ᴗ — —
Is it a phantom of air,--a bodiless, spectral illusion?

— ᴗ ᴗ — ᴗ ᴗ — ᴗ ᴗ — ᴗ ᴗ — ᴗ ᴗ — ᴗ
Is it a ghost from the grave, that has come to forbid the betrothal?

FINAL PROJECT HANDOUT

THE JOURNAL

At the end of this course, you will turn in your journals for grading. You are expected to completely define the vocab, include all the sections required, and present your work neatly.

As it is a journal, minor errors in penmanship are allowed, but efforts must be shown to neaten it up. Crossed out words are fine as long as there is evidence they were corrected.

	Excellent	Good	Fair	Poor
Inclusion of sections	All sections are included (cover page, characters, nautical terms, weaponry, flora & fauna, reflections, and vocab)	There are 1-3 sections missing	There are 4-6 sections missing	There are more than 6 sections missing
Depth of reflections	Reflections take up half a page each, and two are present for each part	Reflections are shorter than half a page	Five or more reflections are missing	Ten or more reflections are missing
Attractiveness & Organization	The journal has exceptionally well-organized information.	The journal has well-organized information.	The journal has some well-organized information.	The journal's organization of material is confusing to the reader.
Bonus points: illustrations	The journal includes a minimum of ten illustrations in the definitions of vocabulary and in some of the reflections	The journal includes a minimum of eight illustrations in the definitions of vocabulary and in some of the reflections	The journal includes a minimum of five illustrations in the definitions of vocabulary and in some of the reflections	The journal includes a minimum of two illustrations in the definitions of vocabulary and in some of the reflections

HOMEWORK

While it is not recommended to offer reflection questions prior to reading the poem's parts, some minor research done ahead of time will benefit students as they encounter the phrases in the poem. Below is a list of suggested assignments for students to do prior to reading each part of the poem. For ease of grading, the students may enter their assignments into their class notebooks. The instructor can either do a quick walk around the classroom to check the entries, or ask for the notebooks in advance of the class meeting for a thorough assessment.

Prior to reading Part One:

- Write two paragraphs on Saint Gregory's historic Latin phrase "NON ANGLI SED ANGELI." Answer the following questions:

    - Why would beautiful people belong in Heaven?

    - What makes someone beautiful?

    - Why should we share our faith with others?

Prior to reading Part Two:

o Write two paragraphs on the Twelfth Legion.

Prior to reading Part Three:

o Look up 1Kings 11:4-5 and write a paragraph on who Astaroth is. You may use approved print sources to supplement this assignment (do not encourage students to use the internet for this assignment since there are suspicious sites on the subject).

Prior to reading part Four:

o For extra credit, since specific knowledge of Herodotus is required, answer the following question: what did Idanthyrsus give to Darius along with five arrows, and what did it signify?

- Answer - A bird, a mouse, a frog, and five arrows. The bird was a warning for him to fly into the air like a bird. The mouse was a warning to hide in the ground like a mouse. The frog was a warning to flee to the water like a frog. The arrows signified the consequence of the challenge: if he didn't flee then he would be destroyed by Scythian arrows.

Prior to reading Part Five:

- Write a paragraph each on the biblical Midianites & Philistines

Prior to reading part Seven:

- Write a paragraph on Bertha the Spinner. Caveat: students will need to plan time to use a library since it requires the use of specialized reference books, and possibly the assistance of a librarian. You can give them a huge hint to help them on their way: she was the mother of Charlemagne.

Prior to reading Part Nine:

- Describe the wedding between Ruth & Boaz from the Book of Ruth 4:10-11

After completing the poem:

o If you were given an unlimited amount of money to produce a series of pictures (paintings, drawings, mixed media, etc) to highlight the poem, which scenes would you select? In this scenario, you may hire any famous or budding artist (living or dead) to carry out the work. Write a paragraph defending your choices, and list out the scenes. Give each scene a title.

DISCUSSION PROMPTS

Students are advised to reflect on the readings before discussing them in class. The following prompts are provided to enhance class discussions. Reflections are intended to be personal and original insights, so it's recommended these prompts are not offered prior to assigning the readings. They are intended to supplement class discussion after students have completed the writing assignment.

Discussion: Part 1

1. Refer to line 24: "Look at these arms . . ." Some people like to point out everything they own with pride. Do the things we own tell others about who we are? Do we sometimes pass judgment on others based on the things they have or don't have?

2. Refer to line 37: "Serve yourself, would you be well served." What does this say about the character of Miles Standish? Is he controlling? Innovative? Does he have a good sense of initiative? Integrity?

3. Miles Standish seems very stern, but he shows a human side. When does he show his human side?

a. Can you see the grave of Rose Standish as a synecdoche for something? Loss of life? The price of war? The risks involved with exploration?

4. Why does Miles Standish find comfort in war books?

5. Standish talks to Alden while the young man is writing. Have you ever been distracted by someone while you tried to study? Have you ever been the one who talks to someone who's trying to get work done? What are some polite responses you could give to someone who interrupts your work?

Discussion: Part 2

1. What does it say about Miles Standish's character when he agrees with Caesar's remark on line 100 about being the first man among Iberians?

2. Do you see foreshadowing in the catalog of Caesar's achievements, ending with betrayal by his friend, Brutus?

3. Refer to lines 96-97. Do you think this is hyperbole? Is it possible for any human to multitask?

4. Refer to lines 130-131: "Speak: for whenever you speak I am always ready to listen . . ." How are these line similar to Samuel's response to God in 1 Samuel 3:10?

Discussion: Part 3

1. Have you ever repented of idolizing someone in the form of a crush like John Alden does? If so, did you accuse yourself of demon worship?

2. Refer to the Gospel of Luke 9:62. What does Jesus mean about looking back?

    a. Refer to lines 245-248 of the poem. How do you feel after reading Alden's thoughts?

3. Refer to line 295: "If I am not worth the wooing, I surely am not worth the winning." Discuss.

4. Why is Priscilla alone in this part? Refer to the cover of this book for a clue.

5. How would you summarize Priscilla's feelings in lines 268-279?

6. Refer to line 285. Did Standish expect Alden to deliver the message in an abrupt manner?

7. Refer to lines 314-334. Are these good arguments to sway Priscilla? If you were in her shoes, would you be convinced to admire Miles Standish?

Discussion: Part 4

1. Refer to line 346. Discuss how the "fading splendor of the sun" is a symbol.

2. Refer to line 421. Is it fair of Standish to compare Alden to Brutus?

3. Refer to line 423. What angers Standish more: Priscilla's rejection, or John's apparent treachery?

4. For those who accepted the extra credit challenge on Darius and the Scythian Prince (refer to the Homework section of this Guide), discus the similarity of this legend with the events in line 454 of Longfellow's poem.

5. Refer to line 476. Would Standish react this way if the council met before Alden returned?

6. What does Standish do with the rattlesnake skin?

    a. Is it a good idea to make any decision in an angry mood?

    b. When you are angry and must make a decision or travel somewhere (e.g. if you have to go to school), what are some things you can do before you make a move?

    c. What would the world be like if people who felt anger stopped for a moment to pray to God to remove their anger and install His love?

Discussion: Part 5

1. Refer to line 562. Is it true that despair is swifter than keel is or canvas?

2. Refer to the book of Genesis 1:2. How is the Mayflower's departure like the creation of the world?

3. Refer to line 555 in the poem. Would you trust a shipmaster with an important verbal message?

4. What are some of the anxieties the pilgrims would have faced regarding the Mayflower's departure?

Discussion: Part 6

1. Refer to line 723. What is the Holy Land of your longings?

2. Refer to line 632. Have you ever given someone the silent treatment? Is it a mature response?

3. What does Priscilla say to bring John to his senses?

Discussion: Part 7

1. Refer to line 739. Why does Standish exhibit sour grapes?

2. Refer to line 760. "Welcome, Englishmen" were the first words spoken to the pilgrims by Chief Samoset from Maine. How did he know this English phrase?

3. Refer to line 818. Imagine seeing the head of Wattawamat on the roof of the church. Are you with Priscilla or the others in your reaction to this?

4. Refer to line 809. What makes this such a powerful line?

    a. Do you feel pity for the Indian?

    b. Does it give you a feeling of pity for all Indians?

        i. You may open a discussion on racism and classism with this. Discuss the current condition of Native Americans and the prejudice and poverty they still face. The finest writers and artists do not create with a political agenda: they are interested in truth, beauty, and goodness. Does Longfellow write with an unbiased voice, looking at both sides equally?

Discussion: Part 8

1. Refer to line 843. Imagine living in a house with paper windows during a thunderstorm and during a rainy day. Free-write on this topic for ten minutes.

2. Refer to lines 857-864 which describe Proverbs' Virtuous Woman (see Proverbs 31:10-31). How is trust related to virtue?

3. In line 901 a tense scene is interrupted by a war messenger. Where else in the poem has a scene been interrupted by a war messenger? Contrast the moods of the two scenes.

4. At the end of this section of the poem, Priscilla and John are happy, even though they've just been warned the town will be burned and all the people will be murdered (line 906). What does this tell you about true love and mortality?

Discussion: Part 9

1. Compare the sunrise (lines 926-931) to the Jewish high priest's garments in Exodus 28.

2. Refer to line 936. Describe Ruth's wedding in the book of Ruth 4: 10-11.

   a. What was Boaz like before he met Ruth?

3. Refer to line 958. Is this the ghost of Miles Standish, or did the messenger make a mistake regarding his death?

4. What is the meaning of line 973: "No man can gather cherries in Kent at the season of Christmas"?

5. Refer to line 988. How does this relate to the Bible's description of Eden in Genesis 2: 8-17?

6. Refer to line 1013. How does this relate to the biblical story in Numbers 13: 23-24?

7. Refer to line 1015. How does this relate to the biblical story of Rebecca and Isaac in Genesis 24?

8. Who is your favorite character after reading the poem? What do you admire in this character?

QUIZZES

The quizzes on the following pages are best administered at the end of the class period to assess student engagement. There is one quiz for each section of the poem. If time allows, instructors may administer supplementary pop quizzes at the beginning of class to cover vocab and content (not included in this guide – such pop quizzes might involve going around the room, orally asking for definitions of random vocab noted in the instructor's own journal, or using the following quizzes themselves as an oral "pre-quiz").

The Courtship of Miles Standish

Quiz 1, covering part 1

1. Where is the poem set?
   a. Denmark
   b. England
   c. America
   d. Flanders

2. What best describes Standish's mannerisms?
   a. Reserved
   b. Relaxed
   c. Martial
   d. Unconfident

3. Who is compared to St. Gregory's Angels?
   a. Priscilla
   b. John
   c. Miles
   d. Squanto

4. Standish likens his howitzer to:
   a. A security guard
   b. A mother bear
   c. A preacher
   d. A soldier

5. Who was the first to die of all who came on the Mayflower?
   a. Priscilla's parents
   b. John's father
   c. Rose Standish
   d. Miles' son

6. Which book does Standish select to comfort his grief?
   a. Barriffe's Artillery Guide
   b. The Commentaries of Caesar
   c. The Federalist Papers
   d. The Bible

7. Why might Alden's letters be full of the name of Priscilla?
   a. She lost her family
   b. She's a good puritan maiden
   c. He is very fond of her
   d. All of the above

8. What is a doublet?
   a. A man's close-fitting jacket
   b. Two lines of rhymed poetry
   c. A small two-sided knife
   d. A type of beer

9. When did the pilgrims settle in Plymouth?
   a. The 1520s
   b. The 1420s
   c. The 1620s
   d. The 1720s

10. Why is Standish's beard flaked with patches of snow?
    a. He has just been shoveling snow
    b. He has just been eating snow
    c. His beard is turning white with age
    d. He and Alden are in a snowball fight

The Courtship of Miles Standish

Quiz 2, covering part 2

1. Who is said to have dictated seven letters at once?
   a. Caesar
   b. Standish
   c. Milton
   d. Alden

2. What happens to Caesar in the end?
   a. He kills his friend
   b. He is stabbed by his friend
   c. He is killed in battle
   d. He passes away in his sleep

3. Standish calls himself a maker of:
   a. Peace
   b. Phrases
   c. War
   d. Weapons

4. Point-blank means:
   a. To aim or fire directly at a mark
   b. A period followed by a space
   c. Fire at will
   d. Hold your fire

5. Where is the Iberian Peninsula?
   a. France
   b. Spain
   c. England
   d. Morocco

6. Where is Flanders?
   a. France
   b. Norway
   c. Belgium
   d. Turkey

7. What is Standish afraid of?
   a. Snakes
   b. Fire
   c. Spiders
   d. Rejection

8. Who does Alden keep writing about?
   a. Standish
   b. Squanto
   c. Weapons
   d. Priscilla

9. What is a maxim?
   a. A short-handled knife
   b. A hunting rifle
   c. A saying
   d. A large piece of armor

10. What is a stripling?
    a. A rooted tree seed
    b. Early American currency
    c. A piece of straw used for thatched roofing
    d. A youth

The Courtship of Miles Standish

Quiz 3, covering part 3

1. What are the aerial cities in the forest?
    a. fairy gardens
    b. tree houses
    c. bird nests
    d. angel dwellings

2. Who is Astaroth?
    a. the crowned prince of hell
    b. a bluebird
    c. A Carthaginian enemy of Caesar
    d. Standish's oldest friend

3. In the forest, Alden feels
    a. conflicted
    b. repentant
    c. disappointed
    d. all of the above

4. Alden accuses himself of:
    a. bearing false witness
    b. worshipping idols of Baal
    c. coveting his neighbor's wife
    d. dishonoring his father

5. Alden delivers the message to Priscilla:
    a. smoothly
    b. eloquently
    c. bluntly
    d. suavely

6. Priscilla is homesick for
    a. Cape Cod
    b. England
    c. Flanders
    d. Amsterdam

7. dilate means
    a. to mix with water
    b. to remove scruples
    c. to cause one to be late
    d. to widen

8. proffer means
    a. to steal
    b. to preen
    c. to offer for acceptance
    d. a fop

9. to reel means:
    a. to sway
    b. to punch
    c. to sail
    d. to bring someone out of a daydream

10. quail means:
    a. to draw back in fear
    b. to whimper
    c. to fail
    d. to flail

The Courtship of Miles Standish
Quiz 4, covering part 4

1. Priscilla's response causes Alden to become
    a. angry at Priscilla
    b. feverish
    c. overjoyed
    d. bored

2. What biblical figure is Priscilla compared to?
    a. Judith
    b. Elizabeth
    c. Delilah
    d. Bathsheba

3. Alden sees the Mayflower and decides:
    a. to rip up the letters he wrote
    b. to catch a ride home with the sailors
    c. to capture Standish and force him to leave with the sailors
    d. to ask Standish nicely to depart with the sailors

4. While Alden was on his errand, Standish had time to:
    a. polish ten weapons
    b. write ten letters
    c. fight ten battles
    d. plant ten seeds

5. Standish handles the news of the errand with
    a. murderous rage
    b. silent lucidity
    c. apathy
    d. soft-spoken acceptance

6. Alden responds to Standish's response by:
    a. weeping
    b. praying
    c. shouting back in anger
    d. snatching a sword

7. At the assembly, Standish finds:
    a. a stern Indian
    b. ten fiddlers
    c. a chandler
    d. a cobbler

8. what is parley?
    a. a type of flower
    b. a type of cannon
    c. a conference between enemies over terms of truce
    d. a whole grain

9. what is a howitzer?
    a. a short cannon
    b. a type of flower
    c. a type of seaweed
    d. a short European jacket

10. who admonishes Standish?
    a. a fiddler
    b. a chandler
    c. a cobbler
    d. a smith

The Courtship of Miles Standish

Quiz 5, covering part 5

1. Hobomok is:
    a. An Indian healer
    b. An Indian guide
    c. A Dutch sailor
    d. The first child to die in the Plymouth Colony

2. Whose feet are on the purple mountain tops?
    a. God's
    b. Hobomok's
    c. The sun's
    d. Samoset's

3. Who is absent when the Mayflower departs?
    a. Alden
    b. Priscilla
    c. Standish
    d. The fiddler

4. With one foot on the Mayflower, Alden sees Priscilla and decides:
    a. To hop onto the ship without looking back
    b. To stay in America
    c. To jump in the ocean and drown
    d. None of the above

5. What mysterious figure is seen on the hill as the Mayflower departs?
    a. A Marian apparition
    b. A Native American
    c. Miles Standish
    d. A Jesuit Missionary

6. What is a pallet?
    a. A bed of straw
    b. A type of flower
    c. A shorebird
    d. A roof of the mouth

7. What is a keel?
    a. An insult
    b. A poetic device
    c. The principal structural member of a ship, running lengthwise along the center line from bow to stern.

8. What are thwarts?
    a. Spiritual talismans used by Native Americans
    b. The chirps of birds
    c. Bubonic pustules on the skin
    d. Seats across a boat on which rowers sit

9. What is a bivouac?
    a. A cow
    b. A military encampment
    c. A short handled knife
    d. A loose-fitting undergarment

10. What is "send" in nautical terms?
    a. To enslave a sailor
    b. A tear in a sail
    c. The smell of rancid fruit on a ship
    d. The lift of a wave

The Courtship of Miles Standish

Quiz 6, covering part 6

1. What is special about loadstone?
    a. It is harder than diamond
    b. It can be used as soap
    c. It is magnetized
    d. It can be turned into gold by alchemists

2. Priscilla cannot _____ what she said to Alden
    a. Undo
    b. Untie
    c. Unsay
    d. Unravel

3. Priscilla says her friendship with Alden is:
    a. Sacred
    b. Trifling
    c. Inconstant
    d. Weak

4. What does subterranean mean?
    a. Underground
    b. A region of southern France
    c. A small sailing vessel
    d. A type of British sandwich

5. Priscilla confesses to John that she likes him more than as a friend
    a. True
    b. False

6. Priscilla compares Standish to a
    a. Powerhouse
    b. Ship
    c. Road
    d. Chimney

7. What does archly mean?
    a. Chiefly
    b. Typically
    c. With playful slyness
    d. Cruelly

8. What is decorum?
    a. Decorations
    b. A type of fabric
    c. Roof thatching
    d. Appropriateness of behavior

9. What does it mean to be affronted?
    a. To be insulted intentionally
    b. To move to the head of the line
    c. To win
    d. To wear an apron

10. What is importunate?
    a. Rude
    b. Troublesomely urgent in requesting
    c. A list of imported goods
    d. A gatekeeper

The Courtship of Miles Standish

Quiz 7, covering part 7

1. What smells sweeter to Standish than the scents of the forest?
    a. The sea
    b. Pages of books
    c. Bread
    d. Gunpowder

2. Who "revolved his discomfort"?
    a. Alden
    b. Hobomok
    c. Standish
    d. The fiddler

3. What does flout mean?
    a. To show contempt
    b. To cook fish
    c. To prance
    d. To sniff

4. Standish vows to become a wooer of:
    a. Women
    b. Dangers
    c. Peace
    d. Books

5. Who taught the Native Americans the phrase, "Welcome, English"?
    a. Alden
    b. Standish
    c. Jesuit missionaries
    d. Traders

6. What does chaffer mean?
    a. To bargain
    b. To scrape
    c. A male heifer
    d. To speak endlessly

7. What are peltries?
    a. Steeples
    b. A type of fish
    c. Fur skins
    d. Fertilizers

8. Wattawamat says he was born:
    a. By being plucked from a rose bush
    b. Of a woman
    c. Of a wolf
    d. From an oak-tree riven by lightning

9. Wattawamat dies clutching:
    a. Wampum
    b. The land of his fathers
    c. His chest
    d. Standish's arm

10. Everyone takes courage from the war trophy except:
    a. Priscilla
    b. John
    c. Hobomok
    d. Standish

The Courtship of Miles Standish

Quiz 8, covering part 8

1. What is a merestead?
   a. A barn
   b. A distinct beard shape
   c. A drink
   d. The land within the boundaries of a farm

2. What is "breaking the glebe"?
   a. Joking with the town fool
   b. Breaking the soil
   c. Raising a toast
   d. Avoiding the plague

3. What material was put in the window-panes?
   a. Waxed paper
   b. Oiled paper
   c. Glass
   d. Mica

4. What is the name of Alden's white bull?
   a. Bucephalus
   b. Rocinante
   c. Raghorn
   d. Blueskin

5. John compares Priscilla to
   a. Rapunzel
   b. Snow White
   c. Brynhild
   d. Bertha the Spinner

6. Who is said to have died in this part?
   a. Standish
   b. Alden
   c. Priscilla
   d. Hobomok

7. What is a palfrey?
   a. A war horse
   b. A riding horse
   c. A type of hat
   d. A type of fish

8. What is a rivulet?
   a. A capsule
   b. A type of skirt
   c. A secret agreement
   d. A small brook

9. What is twain?
   a. One
   b. Two
   c. Three
   d. Four

10. What is a tryst?
    a. A war horse
    b. A sharp point on a weapon
    c. A four-sided shape
    d. A secret agreement between lovers to meet at a certain time and place

The Courtship of Miles Standish

Quiz 9, covering part 9

1. Whose hem has golden bells and pomegranates?
    a. The elder magistrate
    b. Priscilla
    c. Hobomok
    d. The sun

2. The wedding is compared to that of:
    a. Adam & Eve
    b. Ruth & Boaz
    c. Samson & Delilah
    d. Ann & Joachim

3. Who arrives, uninvited, after the wedding?
    a. Wattawamat
    b. Samoset
    c. Hobomok
    d. Standish

4. Priscilla mounts a palfrey named
    a. Raghorn
    b. Tencendur
    c. Samoset
    d. Veillantif

5. As it turns out, Standish didn't die after all.
    a. True
    b. False

6. Gentry is:
    a. An attempt
    b. Verdure
    c. A class of English landowners ranking just below the nobility
    d. A field

7. Commingle means:
    a. To blend thoroughly into a harmonious whole
    b. To arrest
    c. A bird's song
    d. To commit a crime

8. Privation means:
    a. To steal
    b. To kidnap
    c. A ration of food
    d. Lack of the basic necessities of life

9. Tremulous means:
    a. Of a timid disposition
    b. To sing
    c. A bird's song
    d. Precarious

10. What is a threshold?
    a. A wrestling position
    b. Roof beams
    c. A broom
    d. The sill of a doorway

FINAL EXAMINATION

The Courtship of Miles Standish

A. Vocabulary (34 points)

\multicolumn{4}{	l	}{match the number next to the vocab to its definition}
1	martial		heavy or massive
2	fowling-piece		fields
3	russet		to show contempt for
4	azure		musketeer or gunsmith
5	thereof		reduce the intensity of
6	arms		a short cannon
7	arcabucero		easily angered
8	arsenal		greedy for food
9	scout		the heavens
10	ponderous		reddish brown
11	cull		to sway
12	thereupon		to select
13	aghast		of that or it
14	Astaroth		deficient in color
15	ravenous		befitting a warrior
16	pallid		a collection of weapons
17	reel		to draw back in fear
18	quail		to sever
19	ominous		slightly salty water
20	base		menacing, threatening
21	dulse		immediately following that
22	allay		a person sent out to obtain information
23	choleric		to insult intentionally
24	stalwart		weapons
25	howitzer		marked by imposing physical strength
26	ether		a crowned prince of Hell
27	send		a light gun for shooting birds
28	affront		rude
29	flout		the lift of a wave
30	riven		red seaweed
31	glebe		look!
32	brackish		struck with overwhelming shock
33	lo		split
34	sunder		a light, purplish blue

B. Short Answer (66 points)

Answer the following with a minimum of five sentences. Include examples from the poem. Use extra paper if necessary.

In the poem, Miles Standish says if you want something done right, do it yourself. Discuss how this sentiment reflects his character, and how his future defeat is related to this saying.

Miles Standish begins his attack on the Native Americans in a state of anger. Who is he really angry with?

Who is your favorite character in the poem? What do you admire in this character? Include examples.

ANSWER KEY TO QUIZZES

Quiz 1

1. C
2. C
3. B
4. C
5. C
6. B
7. D
8. A
9. C
10. C

Quiz 2

1. A
2. B
3. C
4. A
5. B
6. C
7. D
8. D
9. C
10. D

Quiz 3

1. C
2. A
3. D
4. B
5. C
6. B
7. D
8. C
9. A
10. A

Quiz 4

1. B
2. D
3. B
4. C
5. A
6. B
7. A
8. C
9. A
10. A

Quiz 5

1. B
2. C
3. C
4. B
5. B
6. A
7. C
8. D
9. B
10. D

Quiz 6

1. C
2. C
3. A
4. A
5. A
6. D
7. C
8. D
9. A
10. B

Quiz 7

1. D
2. C
3. A
4. B
5. D
6. A
7. C
8. D
9. B
10. A

Quiz 8

1. D
2. B
3. B
4. C
5. D
6. A
7. B
8. D
9. B
10. D

Quiz 9

1. D
2. B
3. D
4. A
5. A
6. C
7. A
8. D
9. A
10. D

FINAL EXAM ANSWER KEY

1.	10	13.	5	25.	24
2.	31	14.	16	26.	14
3.	29	15.	1	27.	2
4.	7	16.	8	28.	20
5.	22	17.	18	29.	27
6.	25	18.	34	30.	21
7.	23	19.	32	31.	33
8.	15	20.	19	32.	13
9.	26	21.	12	33.	30
10.	3	22.	9	34.	4
11.	17	23.	28		
12.	11	24.	6		

In grading the short answer portion, keep in mind examples must be present. Each short answer is worth 22 points (but you may wish to weight it heavier as an exam).

PROJECTS

To supplement students' learning and engagement with the poem, the following projects are offered.

Projects may be assigned throughout the course, split up according to the knowledge as it is encountered in studying the poem.

Here is the suggested sequence after reading the specified parts:

- Part One: Angel Arcabucero Poster
- Part Two: Spinning Wheel Diagram
- Part Five: Nautical Museum Visit
- Part Seven: Weaponry Slide Presentation
- Part Eight: Map Poster
- Part Nine: Flora & Fauna Collage/Diorama
- Upon completion of the course, students will turn in their journals for a final grade.

The rubrics included in this guide are intended to be distributed to students and handed in along with their projects for grading. The instructor may mark the rubrics to hand back to students to show how their grade is determined.

Additional project ideas are located after the project rubrics.

Project: Angel Arcabucero

In Part 1 of the poem, Miles Standish shows his scribe the bullet-dent in his armor from when he was shot with a Spanish arcabucero.

Around the time of the events depicted in the poem, a new style of religious art was emerging in Peru, based on Spanish and Dutch engravings. This style depicted an angel dressed in Spanish aristocratic clothing who carries an arcabucero instead of a sword. The figure is called "Angel Arcabucero."

Research images of the Angel Arcabucero and create a poster of your own creation either using 17th century Spanish accouterments, or update the clothing and weapon for contemporary times. A contemporary angel might wear a business suit or modern Sunday-dress and carry an automatic pistol.

On the back of the poster, students must include a list of resources they consulted to come up with the image. Also include a sentence or two on why some angels are depicted with a weapon in art.

Extra Credit: some of the depictions of the Angel Arcabucero are that of the apocryphal archangel Uriel. Ask a priest or theologian how the Church views apocryphal figures (e.g. can we ask for their intercession?). Write a short paper on the difference between tradition and Apocrypha, including the difference between venerating Saints Anne & Joachim who do not appear in scripture, and refraining from venerating Saint Uriel.

	Excellent	Good	Fair	Poor
Neatness and Color	The poster is in full color with no white spaces and is presented with exceptional neatness	The poster contains less than 80% color and is neat	The poster contains less than 70% color and is somewhat neat	The poster shows signs of little effort to be neat.
Citations	Sources are cited on the back using an accepted format	Some sources are cited	Few sources are cited	No sources are cited

Project: Nautical Museum Scavenger Hunt

If there is a maritime museum in your area, you may plan a field trip to visit it. In preparation, have the class come to a consensus as to all the nautical terms included in the poem (based on their journal entries up to part 5).

The list should include:

Line 368: "riding at anchor"
Line 368: cordage
Line 560: thwarts
Line 560: keel
Line 593: tiller
Line 593: windlass
Line 607: quarter (quarterdeck)

You may supplement the list with the following terms not specified in the poem:

Bow, Stern, Weather deck, Mast

Once the class has located the terms, provide them with the following worksheet to bring with them to the museum. Be sure to bring a copy of the poem along to discuss context.

At the museum, have students locate pieces that depict all the items on their list. Have them write the title of the museum piece and a brief explanation of where the item can be found in the piece. If they are unable to find some, instruct them to ask the docent to direct them to appropriate pieces (and in preparation for the trip, provide the museum director with the terms as well). If the museum does not include particular items, gather the students together to listen to the docent's description of whatever might be missing. Have students take notes on any such description.

Students will be required to hand in their worksheets for a grade. The first student to locate all the pieces might earn a prize.

Upon return to school, the class should compose a group thank-you letter to the museum director, including the names of the docents who helped them. If they haven't yet mastered the proper form for a personal letter, this is a wonderful teaching opportunity. You may wish to offer a practice-run by way of composing letters to the oldest living person in their family. To make it special, provide stationery for the final drafts, and sealing wax with stamps.

Nautical Museum Worksheet

Locate pieces in the museum that depict the following terms. Write down the title of the piece and where the items listed below can be found in the piece.

Line 368: "riding at anchor"

Line 368: cordage

Line 560: thwarts

Line 560: keel

Line 593: tiller

Line 593: windlass

Line 607: quarter (quarterdeck)

Supplemental terms:
Bow

Stern

Weather deck

Mast

Group Project: Weaponry Slide Presentation

For classrooms that do not have the technology to build PowerPoint, Google Slide, or Prezi presentations, this project may be completed as a series of printed storyboards, or as a booklet.

As a group, create a slide show that displays the various weapons mentioned in the poem. Describe their design and use. Cite sources in a final slide using MLA format (refer to easybib.com). Presentations that copy images from websites must cite the sources of the images within the respective slides. Students may decide how to divide the tasks equally, and must hand in the "Division of Tasks" document (found after the rubric), signed by each student.

Weapons to include (in order of appearance in the poem):

Cutlass	Arsenal	Sabre
Sword of Damascus	Rest	Trenchant knife (AKA trench knife)
Fowling piece	Howitzer	Feathery arrows
Musket	"grounding a musket"	Barb
Matchlock	Hand-grenade	Arrows & bowstrings
Bullet	Scabbard	

Rubric: Weaponry Slide Presentation

Student name _____

	Excellent	Good	Fair	Poor
Presentation	Slides are presented with an engaging delivery – signs of rehearsal are present	Slides are presented with a few supplemental comments to engage the audience	Little signs of rehearsal are demonstrated	Slides are merely read out loud
Mechanics	All spelling and grammar is correct	A minimum of three errors	A minimum of five errors	Six or more errors
Completeness	All weapons are included and are presented knowledgably	Missing three or fewer weapons, or are defined incorrectly	Missing five or fewer weapons, or are defined incorrectly	Missing six or more weapons, or are defined incorrectly
Originality	Obvious efforts to be creative and insightful are demonstrated	Some efforts to be creative and insightful are demonstrated	Few efforts to be creative and insightful are demonstrated	Credit is not given for others' ideas
Sources	All sources are cited properly	Most sources are cited properly	Does not follow MLA format	No citations included

Group Project Division of Tasks

Describe the tasks you performed in the preparation, creation, and presentation of the project. Be sure to include the percentage of work you feel you contributed to the overall project:

Student 1:

Printed name _____

Description of tasks:

Signature _____

Student 2:

Printed name _____

Description of tasks:

Signature _____

Student 3:

Printed name _____

Description of tasks:

Signature _____

Project: Mapmaking

You will create a map on a regular 8 ½ x 11" sheet of paper. Include all the places named in the poem, and follow the criteria outlined in the rubric. Because of the breadth of regions, you may include Middle-Eastern places in a miniature map as a call-out box placed over a neutral area. Include all of the following places:

The Old Colony	Hainault	River Euphrates
Duxbury Hall, Lancashire, England	Brabant	Deserts of Havilah
Flanders	Holland	Jerusalem
Iberia	The point of the Gurnet (AKA Gurnet Point)	Gath
Amsterdam	The field of the First Encounter (AKA the First Encounter)	Bashan
England		Helvetia
	The open Atlantic	
Plymouth		Southampton

Rubric: Map Project

Student name _____

	Excellent	Good	Fair	Poor
Proper identification of places	All regions are identified in their correct areas	16 places are in their correct areas	14 places are in their correct areas	Less than 14 places are in their correct areas
Spelling & Proofreading	There are no spelling mistakes	There are 1-3 spelling mistakes	There are 4-6 spelling mistakes	There are more than 6 spelling mistakes
Color	The entire map is in color, using tan for neutral areas and blue for bodies of water.	80% of the map is in color	70% of the map is in color	The map is not in color
Compass rose, key, and border	All three elements are present	Two elements are present	One element is present	No elements are present
Attractiveness & Neatness	The map has an exceptionally attractive design and is very neat	The map has an attractive design and is neat	The map lacks a thoughtful design and is difficult to read	The map is illegible.

Project: Flora & Fauna

You will create a poster 11" x 14" that includes a minimum of 10 species of flora and fauna found in The Courtship of Miles Standish. The creatures will be labeled and illustrated in color. You may use a cut-and-paste / decoupage technique for this project.

Alternatively, you may create a diorama applying the same criteria to the project.

	Excellent 25 points	Good 21 points	Fair 18 points	Poor 10 points	Nil
Contents	At least 10 species are included.	At least 8 species are included.	the wrong species are included.	Less than 8 species are included.	No species are included
Visual design	At least four colors are included with a title and the student's name	Three colors are included with a title and the student's name	Two colors are included with a title and the student's name	One color is included or no title or no student's name	No color or title or name
Spelling	All words are spelled correctly.	Most words are spelled correctly.	Some words are spelled correctly.	Few words are spelled correctly.	No words are spelled correctly
Effort	Obvious amounts of time and preparation were spent in doing this project.	Some time and preparation were spent in doing this project.	A little time and preparation were spent in doing this project.	This project was completed at 8:00 the morning it was due.	This project does not conform to commonly understood expectations

List of Flora and Fauna found in the poem

(For teacher use only)

line	species
186	robins
186	bluebirds
210	mayflowers
269	hedge-rows
271	lark
271	linnet
274	ivy
350	dulse
350	sea-grass
830	deer
841	firs
842	rushes
850	pennyroyal
848	Raghorn, the snow-white bull
987	Pines
1011	purple grapes

FINAL PROJECT– THE JOURNAL

At the end of this course, you will turn in your journals for grading. You are expected to completely define the vocab, include all the sections required, and present your work neatly.

As it is a journal, minor errors in penmanship are allowed, but efforts must be shown to neaten it up. Crossed out words are fine as long as there is evidence they were corrected.

	Excellent	Good	Fair	Poor
Inclusion of sections	All sections are included (cover page, characters, nautical terms, weaponry, flora & fauna, reflections, and vocab)	There are 1-3 sections missing	There are 4-6 sections missing	There are more than 6 sections missing
Depth of reflections	Reflections take up half a page each, and two are present for each part	Reflections are shorter than half a page	Five or more reflections are missing	Ten or more reflections are missing
Attractiveness & Organization	The journal has exceptionally well-organized information.	The journal has well-organized information.	The journal has some well-organized information.	The journal's organization of material is confusing to the reader.
Bonus points: illustrations	The journal includes a minimum of ten illustrations in the definitions of vocabulary and in some of the reflections	The journal includes a minimum of eight illustrations in the definitions of vocabulary and in some of the reflections	The journal includes a minimum of five illustrations in the definitions of vocabulary and in some of the reflections	The journal includes a minimum of two illustrations in the definitions of vocabulary and in some of the reflections

OTHER OPTIONAL PROJECTS

1. **Geology**: some stones and geological formations are named in the poem. Take students to a quarry, gem shop, or rock museum and arrange with the authorities beforehand to speak specifically on the geology found in the poem. Prepare a list of rocks and earth formations to be used in a scavenger hunt at the quarry or museum. Please note that if this is a goal for your course, an additional section of the journal should be flagged to keep track of geological terms. Some terms to include are: loadstone, chrysolite, jasper, and sapphire.

2. **Spinning Wheel Diagram**: using reliable resources, guide the students in creating diagrams of a spinning wheel using the terms found in the poem (e.g. spindle, treadle, carded wool), and labeling all the parts. If possible, visit a fiber artist who uses an authentic spinning wheel to demonstrate its function.

3. **Field Trip to the Shooting Range**: The colonists were unfamiliar with firearms, and because of their practical need for hunting and self-defense, Miles Standish came with them to offer training based on his military background. Gun safety is tantamount at the shooting range, and a lesson with strict guidance from a licensed professional will encourage respect for safety of self and others. If possible, find a range that offers lessons in firing rifles. As the students engage in the activity of shooting, remind them of the physical exertion required by the colonists as they went through a similar learning procedure. At the end of the outing, gather together to say a prayer of thanksgiving for the brave men and women who developed the skills needed to survive. Give thanks for their fortitude, their perseverance, and their willingness to learn. Without their efforts, many of us would never have been born.

4. **Look Book:** create a fashion designer's portfolio of all the clothing described in the poem. Point the students to reliable sources for their research. If you have access to a seamstress for guidance, sew pieces of clothing to be presented at a fashion show, with students acting as models walking down a runway. You may include the armor found in the poem using papier-mâché or some such technique.

5. **Meet the Native Americans:** visit an Indian reservation. Ask students to prepare meaningful questions for the people they meet. See if anyone on the rez can demonstrate how people fished in the 17th century.

6. **Field Book of Flora:** in lieu of the collage project, for every plant, tree, and flower in the poem, have students research their scientific names and create charts of their biological parts.

7. **Class Trip to Restored House:** tour a museum house restored to the period of either the colonists, or Longfellow's lifetime. Students will prepare two questions for the docents about the lifestyle of people from the historic time-period. Deliver hand-written thank-you notes to the director of the house after the trip, specifying students' favorite parts of the tour, and expressing gratitude to the tour guide.

    a. If geographically possible, visit the Longfellow House in Portland, Maine

8. **Try Hexameter**: have students create their own poems using dactylic hexameter.

9. **Memorize it**: learn and recite the passage that includes Priscilla's famous retort – lines 333 to 338 that begins with "Any woman in Plymouth . . .".

10. **Wampum Belt**: if your school or academic network includes younger children, consider working with the teachers of elementary age students to prepare them for reading Longfellow when they reach high school. This is the classical model of education: presenting students with palatable amounts of learning which increases cyclically as they grow older. Using a craft book, develop instructions for creating a wampum belt out of noodles and string. Reflect on the value of wampum, and the effort required for small embellishments. Then discuss the obligation of Catholics to tithe in terms of time, treasure, and talent. You may choose to host a "fashion night" to go along with the "Look Book" project (found in this list) of the older students, wherein both levels of students present their work to the community in the style of models on a runway.

FINAL THOUGHTS

To conclude the course, you may wish to invite a history teacher to lecture on the historic figure of Miles Standish, or invite a member of your local chapter of the Mayflower Society to give a talk to the students.

Encourage students to keep their journals as a prototype for future books they wish to read as a deep study. This guidebook is part of a series which follows the same method of journal keeping.

You might distribute evaluation forms when the course concludes, or take an oral poll on whether the students either enjoyed the work or gained enrichment from it. Art is a matter DE GUSTIBUS, a matter of taste, and not every student will love the dactylic hexameter or the subject. The more poetry students are exposed to, the better they form their sense of taste. In my classroom experience, even students who don't find the poem itself appealing will reap some benefits from the study activities. These benefits manifest themselves in feelings of achievement, and fellowship with their peers. My students have reported positive remarks on the course. Even those who wouldn't have enjoyed the book on their own tell me that reading it deeply brings them a new dimension of understanding and appreciation. For students who do enjoy Longfellow, this course offers innumerable pleasures.

May this guidebook help you bring out the Truth, Beauty, and Goodness in the poem.

ABOUT THE AUTHOR

Sarah Yasin is one of the original teachers at Alcuin Academy, a private, independent classical school in the Catholic tradition. This guide is a tool she uses in the classroom for literature seminars. For more information on classical schools, visit NAPCIS.org

Made in the USA
Columbia, SC
03 November 2023